A Note to

DK READERS is a compr... readers, designed in conju... experts, including Dr. Lin... Education at Clemson Ur... served as President of the... the College Reading Assc... Reading Association.

Beautiful illustrations and superb full-color photographs combine with engaging, easy-to-read stories and informational texts to offer a fresh approach to each subject in the series. Each DK READER is guaranteed to capture a child's interest while developing his or her reading skills, general knowledge, and love of reading.

The five levels of DK READERS are aimed at different reading abilities, enabling you to choose the books that are exactly right for your child:

Pre-level 1: Learning to read
Level 1: Beginning to read
Level 2: Beginning to read alone
Level 3: Reading alone
Level 4: Proficient readers

The "normal" age at which a child begins to read can be anywhere from three to eight years old. Adult participation through the lower levels is very helpful for providing encouragement, discussing storylines, and sounding out unfamiliar words.

No matter which level you select, you can be sure that you are helping your child learn to read, then read to learn!

LONDON, NEW YORK,
MELBOURNE, MUNICH, AND DELHI

For DK/BradyGames
Global Strategy Guide Publisher
Mike Degler
Digital and Trade Category Publisher
Brian Saliba
Editor-In-Chief
H. Leigh Davis
Licensing Manager
Christian Sumner
Operations Manager
Stacey Beheler
Title Manager
Tim Fitzpatrick
Book Designer
Tim Amrhein
Production Designer
Tracy Wehmeyer

For DK Publishing
Publishing Director
Beth Sutinis
Licensing Editor
Nancy Ellwood
Reading Consultant
Linda B. Gambrell, Ph.D.

For WWE
Director, Home Entertainment & Books
Dean Miller
Photo Department
Frank Vitucci, Joshua Tottenham, Jamie Nelsen
Copy Editor Kevin Caldwell
Legal Lauren Dienes-Middlen

DK/BradyGAMES
800 East 96th St., 3rd floor
Indianapolis, IN 46240

11 12 13 10 9 8 7 6 5 4 3 2 1

A catalog record for this book is available from the Library of Congress.

ISBN: 978-0-7566-7605-6 (Paperback)

ISBN: 978-0-7566-8704-5 (Hardback)

Printed and bound by Lake Book

The publisher would like to thank the following for their kind
permission to reproduce their photographs:
All photos courtesy WWE Entertainment, Inc.
All other images © Dorling Kindersley
For further information see: www.dkimages.com

Discover more at
www.dk.com

DK READERS

BEGINNING 2 TO READ ALONE

Hornswoggle®

Written by Kevin Sullivan

DK Publishing

In a world dominated by giants, one pint-sized Superstar somehow always manages to shine bright. That Superstar is Hornswoggle.

Since his debut in May 2006, Hornswoggle has shown time and time again that he has the heart and desire to be one of WWE's most popular Superstars. However, it hasn't been an easy road for the little man. At half the height of most Superstars, many believed Hornswoggle was nothing more than a sideshow act.

Years later, he has proven the doubters wrong, claiming his place in many memorable moments, including the search for his true father and an unbelievable Cruiserweight Championship reign.

Hornswoggle's Stats
- **Height:** 4'4" (1.32 m)
- **Weight:** 129 pounds (58.5 kg)
- **Signature Move:** Tadpole Splash
- **Debut:** May 26, 2006

Here comes a Tadpole Splash!

The WWE Universe first saw Hornswoggle when he popped out from under the ring after a match between Finlay and Paul Burchill on *SmackDown*. Judging from his green leprechaun attire, it wasn't hard to figure out that he was there to help the Irish Superstar, Finlay. Hornswoggle attacked Burchill repeatedly before Finlay finally stuffed him back under the ring.

Hornswoggle emerges from under the ring!

With Burchill on the mat, Finlay rounds up Hornswoggle!

Hornswoggle just wants to help!

What is a Leprechaun?
A leprechaun is a little man described in Irish fairytales. He is usually seen creating mischief.

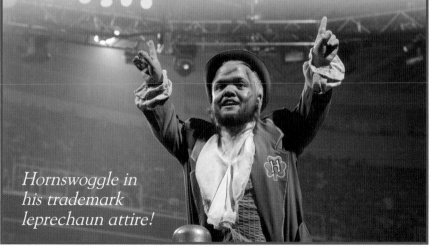

Hornswoggle in his trademark leprechaun attire!

Over the next few weeks, Hornswoggle kept attacking Finlay's opponents. He even helped the Irishman defeat Bobby Lashley for the United States Championship. The win came after Hornswoggle tossed a shillelagh to his pal. Finlay then used the stick to strike down the much bigger Lashley. The new champ held the title for close to two months, thanks in part to Hornswoggle's constant interference.

Finlay gives Bobby Lashley the stick—Hornswoggle's shillelagh!

Finlay hoists his United States Championship title!

What is a Shillelagh?

A shillelagh is a wooden walking stick with a large knob at the top.

Hornswoggle returns to the ring, carrying his shillelagh!

As usual, Hornswoggle again interfered in Finlay's match at *WrestleMania 23*. This time, it was a Money in the Bank Ladder Match, which was much more dangerous than a normal match. During the contest, Hornswoggle tried to climb the ladder, but was caught by Mr. Kennedy.

Hornswoggle makes a break for the briefcase!

Mr. Kennedy thwarts Hornswoggle's attempt!

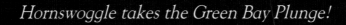

Hornswoggle takes the Green Bay Plunge!

The much bigger Superstar put Hornswoggle on his shoulders and delivered his Green Bay Plunge signature move from the top of the ladder. The move led many to believe Hornswoggle had no business in the ring with Superstars twice his size, but the pint-sized Superstar was about to prove them all wrong.

At *The Great American Bash* in July 2007, Hornswoggle did the unthinkable when he hit Jamie Noble with the Tadpole Splash to become Cruiserweight Champion. With the win, Hornswoggle became the shortest Superstar ever to hold a WWE title.

Hornswoggle unleashes a Tadpole Splash on Jamie Noble!

Noble takes a pie to the face!

Embarrassed by the loss, Noble spent the
next few weeks trying to gain revenge
from Hornswoggle. However, the little
champion always managed to come
out on top. He even threw a pie in
Noble's face and sprayed him with a
fire extinguisher.

Hornswoggle never lost the Cruiserweight Championship. He proudly held the title until September 2007 when Vickie Guerrero stripped him of the gold during her first official night as *SmackDown* General Manager. The title hasn't been seen since, making Hornswoggle the final Cruiserweight Champion in WWE history.

Vickie Guerrero strips Hornswoggle of his title!

Is Hornswoggle Mr. McMahon's son?

In the summer of 2007, it was revealed that WWE Chairman Mr. McMahon had a son on the WWE roster that he didn't know about. Fans immediately began guessing which Superstar could be the newest member of the McMahon family. Many thought it was Mr. Kennedy or even John Cena, but it wasn't. After weeks of guessing, it was finally announced that Hornswoggle was Mr. McMahon's son.

At first, being a McMahon appeared to be a great opportunity for Hornswoggle. Many even compared it to winning the lottery.

However, Hornswoggle soon found out that being the son of Mr. McMahon wasn't what it was cracked up to be. As a way to show tough love to his little son, Mr. McMahon began to put Hornswoggle in impossible matches against bigger and better competitors, such as The Great Khali and William Regal.

Hornswoggle takes his lumps from The Great Khali!

Finlay stayed by Hornswoggle's side during his battles against Mr. McMahon's hand-picked opponents. Even though the competition was strong and mighty, Finlay was always there to lend a hand. It was becoming clear that the two Superstars shared a bond that couldn't be broken.

Finlay and Hornswoggle become great friends!

*Finlay, chained to the cage, is forced to watch
Mr. McMahon and JBL punish his friend!*

During a Steel Cage Match between
Hornswoggle and Mr. McMahon, Finlay
again tried to help the smaller Superstar.
However, John "Bradshaw" Layfield
stopped Finlay and handcuffed him to
the ring. There was nothing he could
do to help. Finlay was forced to watch
helplessly as Mr. McMahon and JBL
punished poor Hornswoggle.

Shortly after the attack, JBL revealed that Hornswoggle was not actually Mr. McMahon's son. The whole situation was just a plan by the McMahon family and Finlay as a way to embarrass Mr. McMahon. It was then revealed that Finlay was Hornswoggle's true father all along.

Finlay is Hornswoggle's father after all!

Hornswoggle and Finlay team up against John Morrison and The Miz!

The father-and-son duo of Finlay and Hornswoggle were inseparable over the course of the next year. They even competed in tag team matches together, beating many teams including John Morrison & The Miz, Zack Ryder & Curt Hawkins, and Tyson Kidd & Natalya.

Hornswoggle's Favorite Moves

- Tadpole Splash
- Sweet Shin Music
- Celtic Cross
- Stunner
- Hornswogglecanrana
- Little Attitude Adjustment
- Senton Bomb

*Hornswoggle and Chavo Guerrero
face off in a boxing match!*

The popular father-
son combination was
split up in April 2009
when Hornswoggle was
sent to *Raw* in the annual WWE Draft.
Despite no longer having his father
by his side, Hornswoggle gained great
success in the *Raw* ring. His main victim
was Chavo Guerrero.

Nearly every week for several months, Hornswoggle and Chavo Guerrero were placed in a different specialty match. The contests turned out to be Guerrero's worst nightmare, as Hornswoggle managed to win each and every week.

Mark Henry plays the role of Hornswoggle!

Hornswoggle hogties Chavo Guerrero in their Texas Bullrope Match!

Hornswoggle vs. Chavo Guerrero Specialty Matches

- July 13, 2009: Hornswoggle defeated Guerrero (Guerrero had one hand tied behind his back)

- July 20, 2009: Hornswoggle defeated Guerrero (Sharp Dressed Man Tuxedo Match)

- July 27, 2009: Hornswoggle defeated Guerrero (Guerrero was blindfolded)

- Aug. 3, 2009: Markswoggle defeated Guerrero (Mark Henry filled in for Hornswoggle)

- Aug. 17, 2009: Hornswoggle defeated Guerrero (Falls Count Anywhere Match)

- Aug. 24, 2009: Hornswoggle defeated Guerrero (Boxing Match)

- Aug. 31, 2009: Hornswoggle defeated Guerrero (Texas Bullrope Match)

Toward the end of 2009, Hornswoggle mysteriously began to wear DX gear. The move confused Shawn Michaels and Triple H, who sent Hornswoggle legal notice to stop wearing their merchandise. However, he refused to listen. Instead, at the advice of actor Verne Troyer, Hornswoggle turned around and sued DX. He even brought them to "Little People's Court."

At first, Triple H and Shawn Michaels tried to make Hornswoggle stop wearing DX gear!

Hornswoggle takes DX to "Little People's Court!"

The legal matter forced HBK and The Game to have a change of heart. In fact, they even accepted Hornswoggle into their legendary faction as the official mascot of DX. As mascot, Hornswoggle mainly escorted Michaels and Triple H to the ring and goofed around with them backstage.

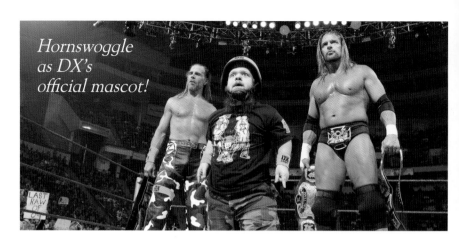

Hornswoggle as DX's official mascot!

The highlight of Hornswoggle's time with DX came when he teamed with his new buddies to defeat The Miz, Big Show, and actor Jon Heder in a Six-Man Tag Team Match on *Raw*.

Hornswoggle drops in on Big Show and Jon Heder!

Hornswoggle was shipped back to *SmackDown* in the April 2010 WWE Draft. Upon arrival, he teamed with Christian to defeat Dolph Ziggler and old foe Chavo Guerrero. The win proved that Hornswoggle could be successful against any sized Superstar on any brand. He even proved he could shine on the major pay-per-view stage when he lasted nearly ten minutes in the 2011 *Royal Rumble.*

Hornswoggle and Christian take it to Chavo Guerrero and Dolph Ziggler!

During the match, he delivered a thrilling Attitude Adjustment to Tyson Kidd and teamed with John Cena to give a double Five Knuckle Shuffle to Heath Slater.

"You can't see me!"

John Cena watches Hornswoggle deliver an Attitude Adjustment!

Despite his small size, Hornswoggle continually demonstrates that he is one of WWE's most popular and successful personalities. Whether he's hiding under the ring, delivering his trademark Tadpole Splash, or hanging out with DX, you can bet Hornswoggle is putting smiles on the faces of the WWE Universe, both young and old.

Hornswoggle is no stranger to victory in the ring!

Hornswoggle Facts

• Hornswoggle eliminated The Miz from the 2008 *Royal Rumble.*

• Hornswoggle competed in the 2008 *King of the Ring* tournament. He lost to William Regal in the first round.

• Hornswoggle was the official mascot of Team SmackDown at *Bragging Rights* 2010.

Hornswoggle as Team SmackDown's mascot!

• Hornswoggle defeated Jack Swagger's Soaring Eagle in one-on-one action in December 2010.

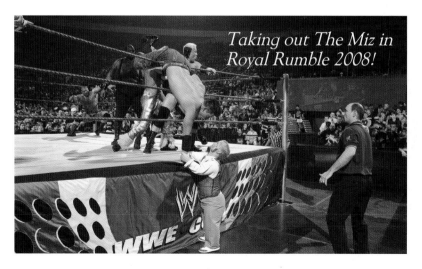

Taking out The Miz in Royal Rumble 2008!